I0446315

HOW TO OPEN AN
APPLIANCE
STORE

A Comprehensive Guide to Starting, Running and
Growing a Successful Home Appliance Retail Business

MORRIS WILLIS

TABLE OF CONTENTS

Introduction

Venturing into the realm of launching an appliance store is like setting out on an exciting entrepreneurial adventure. This book serves as your trusty guide, packed with practical insights and strategies, to navigate the intricate path of establishing and steering a prosperous appliance retail business.

From shaping your store's vision to choosing the perfect location, curating a compelling inventory, and fostering enduring customer bonds, each chapter unveils the essential steps and savvy tactics needed for success in this competitive market. You'll dive deep into supplier relationships, financial management, marketing tricks, and the smart strategies that keep you ahead in an ever-evolving industry.

Beyond just profits, the allure lies in becoming a valued hub within your community—a place where homeowners, DIY enthusiasts, and pros find not just tools but the support and guidance to bring their projects to life. In these chapters, you'll find not just practical advice, but the heart of what it means to build a business that goes beyond transactions, forging lasting connections and becoming a vital part of your customers' lives.

So, gear up your entrepreneurial spirit, arm yourself with determination, and embark on this enlightening journey through these pages. Each turn opens new doors, guiding you toward fulfilling your dream of not just opening but excelling in the world of appliance retail.

Why Start an appliance Store?

Opening an appliance store presents a world of possibilities, each promising its own rewards. Firstly, appliances are the backbone of modern living—be it kitchen essentials like fridges and stoves or household must-haves like washers and TVs. The constant demand ensures a steady flow of customers, offering a solid base for your business to thrive upon. But appliances are more than just necessities; they've become lifestyle statements. Consumers seek products that not only serve their needs but also align with their tastes in style, technology, and sustainability. As a store owner, you have the chance to curate a lineup that caters to diverse preferences, giving you an edge in the market.

Profitability is another enticing aspect. While the startup costs might be significant, the margins in the appliance industry can be quite attractive. Add services like installation, maintenance, and extended warranties, and you've got multiple revenue streams at your disposal.

The ever-evolving tech scene offers exciting opportunities too. Smart appliances, IoT integrations, and eco-friendly solutions are the new frontiers in the industry. Staying updated with these innovations allows your store to be a go-to hub for cutting-edge technology, drawing in tech enthusiasts.

Beyond the business aspect, owning an appliance store lets you contribute to your community. Outfitting new homes or helping folks upgrade their spaces makes your store an essential resource in the neighborhood, building relationships and earning trust as a reliable source for quality appliances.

Starting an appliance store isn't just about commerce—it's about diving into an ever-evolving industry, embracing innovation, and becoming a vital part of people's lives while crafting a thriving business.

Is an appliance Store Right for You?

Opening an appliance store can be an enticing prospect, but before diving into the world of retail, it's crucial to assess whether this endeavor aligns with your interests, strengths, and aspirations. Consider your passion and knowledge in the appliance industry. Are you fascinated by the latest technological innovations, trends, and advancements in household appliances? An inherent interest in these products can serve as a solid foundation for success. A genuine enthusiasm will not only fuel your motivation but also resonate with customers, fostering trust and credibility in your expertise.

Then, evaluate your entrepreneurial spirit and business acumen. Running an appliance store demands more than just a love for gadgets; it requires strategic planning, financial management skills, and a keen understanding of retail operations. Are you prepared to handle the complexities of inventory management, pricing strategies, and customer service? Building and sustaining a profitable business involves meticulous attention to these facets.

Assess the market demand and competition in your area. Conduct thorough market research to gauge the need for an appliance store in your chosen location. Analyze the demographics, consumer behavior, and existing competitors. Identifying gaps or opportunities in the market can provide a clearer picture of the feasibility and potential success of your store.

Financial readiness is another crucial aspect to contemplate. Starting and maintaining an appliance store involves significant initial investment and ongoing operational costs. Do you have access to the necessary capital or financing options to cover expenses such as inventory procurement, store lease, utilities, and staffing?

Furthermore, reflect on your commitment and readiness for the long haul. Launching an appliance store isn't just about the grand opening; it's a continuous journey that requires dedication, adaptability, and resilience. Are you prepared for the challenges and fluctuations inherent in the retail industry? Are you ready to evolve with evolving consumer preferences and technological advancements?

The decision to open an appliance store hinges on a blend of passion, business acumen, market understanding, financial preparedness, and a willingness to dedicate yourself to the venture. Carefully weighing these factors will help you ascertain if an appliance store is indeed the right path for you, setting the stage for a successful and fulfilling entrepreneurial journey.

Chapter 1:
The Appliance Store Industry

The appliance store industry stands as a dynamic and vital part of the retail world, serving the diverse needs of consumers seeking solutions for their homes and technology needs. These stores are go-to spots offering a wide array of appliances, ranging from essential kitchen items like refrigerators and stoves to state-of-the-art smart home gadgets and entertainment systems.

What defines the essence of this industry is its ability to adapt and respond to changing consumer demands and technological advancements. In a world where convenience, efficiency, and innovation matter, these stores continuously update their offerings to include the latest trends and advancements. Whether it's energy-saving appliances or the newest smart devices, the industry aims to improve consumers' lives while catering to their various needs.

Appliance stores operate on multiple fronts, serving both households and commercial sectors. Aside from individual homes, these stores cater to businesses, contractors, and industries needing specialized appliances and equipment. They assist in outfitting professional kitchens, providing tools for construction projects, and supplying appliances for commercial spaces, extending their reach far beyond just home appliances.

Customer service and expertise are the backbone of these stores. Knowledgeable staff members, well-versed in various appliances' features and functionalities, play a crucial role in guiding customers through their purchases. They offer insights on energy efficiency, product comparisons, and installation advice, elevating the overall shopping experience and building trust among customers.

The industry is also influenced by the digital shift, with many stores integrating online platforms and e-commerce alongside their physical presence. This transformation enhances accessibility, convenience, and reach, appealing to customers who prefer online shopping or seek information before visiting the store.

Despite the growth of online retail and large home improvement centers, appliance stores remain resilient due to their personalized service, expert advice, and the tangible experience of interacting with products. They embody reliability, trust, and community connections, nurturing lasting relationships with customers while continuously adapting to meet their changing needs and preferences.

Understanding the Appliance Market

Understanding the appliance market involves delving into a multifaceted landscape shaped by consumer behaviors, technological innovations, economic trends, and industry dynamics. This market encompasses a wide array of products, ranging from everyday household essentials to cutting-edge smart devices, catering to various consumer segments and needs.

Consumer preferences play a pivotal role in shaping the appliance market. Factors such as functionality, energy efficiency, design aesthetics, and technological advancements heavily influence purchasing decisions. For instance, there's a growing demand for appliances equipped with smart features that offer convenience, connectivity, and energy-saving capabilities, aligning with the trend toward interconnected smart homes.

Economic factors also significantly impact the appliance market. Market fluctuations, disposable income, housing trends, and interest rates influence consumers' willingness to invest in big-ticket items like appliances. During economic downturns,

10

consumers may opt for more budget-friendly or essential purchases, while economic upswings might lead to increased spending on higher-end, technologically advanced appliances.

Technological innovation continues to be a driving force within the appliance market. Advancements such as Internet of Things (IoT) integration, artificial intelligence, and energy-efficient technologies shape the landscape, offering enhanced functionalities and improved user experiences. Appliances that contribute to sustainability and environmental conservation are gaining traction among eco-conscious consumers, influencing market trends.

Moreover, the appliance market is segmented to cater to diverse consumer needs and preferences. It encompasses various categories such as kitchen appliances, laundry appliances, home comfort appliances, entertainment electronics, and more. Each segment targets specific consumer demographics and lifestyles, leading to a wide array of products tailored to different market niches.

Retail channels also play a crucial role in the appliance market. Traditional brick-and-mortar stores, online retailers, department stores, specialty appliance shops, and home improvement centers all contribute to the distribution of appliances. The evolving landscape includes omnichannel approaches, where retailers integrate both physical stores and online platforms to provide a seamless shopping experience for consumers.

Additionally, factors like government regulations, industry standards, and sustainability initiatives impact product development and market trends. Increasing regulations regarding energy efficiency and environmental impact drive manufacturers to innovate and produce appliances that meet stringent criteria, influencing consumer choices and market dynamics.

Understanding the appliance market involves a comprehensive grasp of these interconnected factors, allowing stakeholders—from manufacturers and retailers to consumers—to navigate the landscape effectively. By staying attuned to evolving consumer needs, technological advancements, economic shifts, and industry trends, businesses can position themselves strategically within this dynamic market.

What Sets an appliance Store Apart

An appliance store stands out amidst the retail landscape due to several distinguishing factors that set it apart in the eyes of consumers. To begin, personalized service and expertise form the cornerstone of an appliance store's identity. Unlike larger retail chains, these stores often boast a team of knowledgeable staff who possess in-depth understanding and insights into various appliances. Customers benefit from tailored advice, recommendations, and product knowledge, fostering a sense of trust and confidence in their purchase decisions. Also, the range of offerings and specialized inventory available at appliance stores distinguishes them from general retailers. These stores curate a diverse selection of appliances, from basic necessities to high-end, innovative products. This wide array caters to specific needs and preferences, providing customers with options that align with their requirements, whether it's for a small DIY project or a major home renovation.

Beyond the products themselves, the ambiance and shopping experience contribute significantly to setting appliance stores apart. Many of these stores prioritize creating a welcoming and informative atmosphere. Customers often find themselves in spaces where they can interact with appliances, test functionalities, and seek advice from experts, fostering a more engaging and enjoyable shopping journey.

The emphasis on after-sales services and support further distinguishes appliance stores. Beyond the point of purchase, these stores offer installation services, warranties, and maintenance guidance. This commitment to post-purchase assistance adds value to the customer experience, enhancing satisfaction and building long-term relationships.

Community engagement also plays a role in setting appliance stores apart. These stores often actively participate in local events, workshops, and initiatives, fostering a sense of community. Additionally, their localized presence allows them to better understand and cater to the unique needs of their specific customer base.

In an era dominated by online shopping, the tangible experience of visiting an appliance store remains invaluable. The ability to physically interact with appliances, seek advice in person, and receive immediate assistance contributes to the enduring appeal of these stores.

What truly sets an appliance store apart is its ability to combine expertise, personalized service, diverse inventory, engaging shopping experiences, and community connections. This holistic approach not only meets the immediate needs of customers but also fosters enduring relationships, making these stores a vital and trusted resource in the world of retail.

Passion and Vision

Passion and vision are the cornerstone for launching and nurturing a successful appliance store. Passion fuels the entrepreneurial spirit, driving the commitment to providing exceptional service and a diverse inventory of quality tools and materials. It's the deep enthusiasm for catering to the needs of DIY enthusiasts, contractors, and homeowners that propels the business forward, even during challenging times.

Vision, in the context of an appliance store, involves a clear roadmap outlining the store's objectives, target market, and service offerings. It's about envisioning the appliance store as a hub within the community, not merely as a retail space but as a knowledge center, offering expert advice and a diverse range of products. This vision encompasses the store's role in providing solutions, fostering customer relationships, and becoming a trusted resource for all things related to purchase and maintenance.

The fusion of passion and vision in launching an appliance store creates a vibrant atmosphere. It fuels the commitment to quality products, expert guidance, and exceptional customer service. This drive allows the store to cater to the community's needs, offering not just tools and materials but also expertise and a welcoming environment where customers feel valued and understood.

Moreover, this blend of passion and vision attracts like-minded individuals—enthusiastic staff who share the same dedication to serving customers and contributing positively to the community. It encourages teamwork and a shared commitment to the store's mission, fostering a culture of excellence and innovation.

Ultimately, in the realm of starting an appliance store, passion fuels the enthusiasm to embark on this journey, while vision provides the strategic direction and purpose necessary to establish a store that stands out as a trusted and indispensable resource within the community.

Chapter 2:
Market Research and Planning

In the world of business, the phrase "knowledge is power" couldn't be more accurate. Before embarking on the journey of starting your own appliance store, you need to arm yourself with a deep understanding of your market and a well-thought-out plan. This chapter is all about laying the groundwork for your appliance store venture, and it starts with four key components: Understanding Your Target Market, Choosing the Right Location, Competitive Analysis, and Creating a Business Plan.

Understanding Your Target Market

Understanding who your customers are is key for any appliance store aiming to do well in a crowded market. It's all about digging into details like who's buying, what they like, how they shop, and what they really need. You've got to know the basic details about your customers—things like how old they are, where they live, how much they earn, and what their lifestyle looks like. That helps you figure out what kind of appliances they're after. Young city dwellers might want gadgets that fit in small spaces and come with smart features, while families in the suburbs might need bigger, family-friendly appliances.

How people shop and what they prefer in appliances is also super important. Some folks really care about saving energy and want eco-friendly appliances, while others just want the latest tech and convenience. Getting to the nitty-gritty of what your customers really need or what bugs them about their current appliances is crucial too. Talking to them, doing surveys, and checking out what they're saying online can help you spot gaps in the market and offer solutions that hit the mark for them.

Then there's how you talk to them. Whether it's through social media, emails, or events in your store, you've got to reach out in ways that match how your customers like to connect. It's all about building trust and making sure they feel like you get them.

Keeping an eye on trends and changes in what your customers want is also key. The folks you're targeting aren't always the same, so it's important to keep tweaking and updating what you offer and how you talk to them based on what's new and what they're into.

Understanding your customers—knowing who they are, what they want, and how they want it—helps you tailor everything from your products to your marketing to give them what they're looking for.

Choosing the Right Location

Once you've got a good handle on who your appliance store customers are, the next big step is finding the perfect spot to set up shop. Where you place your store matters a lot, and here's why it's so crucial:

Visibility and Easy Access: You want your store to be super easy to spot and get to. The best places usually have lots of people passing by and are near where people live, making it convenient for shoppers to find and reach your store.

Checking Out the Competition: Figuring out who else is selling appliances nearby is a must. Are there other stores doing what you do? What makes your store special? Spotting where there's room for you to stand out is key.

Matching the People: Your store location should match up with the kind of folks you want to attract. For example, if your store's in an area with lots of families, you might focus on good deals, while if it's near health-conscious people, you might go for more eco-friendly products.

Following the Rules: Paying attention to local rules and permits is a big deal. These things can affect how your store looks, when it's open, and what you can sell. Making sure you're on the right side of the law is important for a successful business.

Counting the Costs: Thinking about how much it's going to cost you to set up shop in a certain place is crucial. Rent, bills, upkeep—those things add up. You want to make sure your spot will make enough money to cover all that. Doing some number crunching is a must.

Getting some help from a real estate pro who knows about retail spaces can be a big help. They can guide you to places that match what you're after, help with lease stuff, and make sure the spot you pick is a plus for your business, not a minus.

Choosing the right spot for your appliance store sets the stage for success. A good location can bring in customers, help you stand out from the competition, and make strong connections with the people you want to reach. By thinking about these things and getting some expert advice, you can pick a spot that'll set your store up for big wins in the busy retail world.

Competitive Analysis

Understanding your competition is essential for standing out in the appliance store industry. Doing a comprehensive analysis helps you navigate this complex world by spotting strengths, weaknesses, opportunities, and threats. Here's how to tackle this crucial task:

First, make a detailed list of all the appliance stores in your area. But don't stop there—include nearby convenience stores, supermarkets, and even online options that could compete with you. The broader your view, the better your understanding.

For each competitor, do a SWOT analysis. Figure out their Strengths, like unique products or a strong brand. Look at their Weaknesses, like poor service or limited choices. Find the Opportunities they might be missing, like new markets. And don't forget to check the Threats they face, like new competitors. This gives you a clear picture of your competition.

Now, find what makes your store special. Your Unique Selling Proposition (USP) could be anything from offering organic products to top-notch service or exclusive in-store experiences. Your USP is what draws customers to you.

Look at how your competitors price their stuff. Are they targeting high-end buyers or budget shoppers? Find your spot—your pricing should match your target customers and your USP. It's all about balancing competitiveness and profit.

If you can, get your hands on market share data for your area. It tells you who's ruling the market and where there might be gaps. Even if a competitor has a big piece of the market, there might still be areas they're not covering well.

This analysis helps you create a roadmap for your store's success. It paints a clear picture of your market, spots chances to grow, and shows where you can shine. By understanding your competitors' strengths, weaknesses, and opportunities, you can fine-tune your plan, make a winning strategy, and set your store up for long-term success in a tough market.

Crafting a Comprehensive Business Plan

Now that you've gained a profound understanding of your target market, selected an optimal location, and gleaned insights into your competition, it's time to synthesize all this valuable information into a structured business plan. A business plan is your blueprint for steering your appliance store toward success. It encompasses several key components, each contributing to the overall framework of your vision:

Executive Summary: At the forefront of your business plan is the executive summary. This concise section encapsulates your business's essence, featuring your mission statement, overarching goals, and a summary of your financial forecasts.

Company Description: Dive deep into the intricacies of your appliance store in the company description section. Paint a vivid picture of your venture, elucidating your vision, the array of products you intend to offer, your unique selling propositions, and the profile of your target market.

Market Analysis: Summarize the insights gleaned from your thorough market research. Include pertinent details about your target market's demographics, the strategic choice of your location, and the competitive landscape you've uncovered.

Organization and Management: Provide an organizational blueprint. Who comprises your key team members, and what roles will they fulfill? Highlight relevant experience and qualifications that bolster your team's ability to execute your business strategy.

Products and Services: Outline an exhaustive list of the products and services that your appliance store will provide. Elaborate on any distinctive or specialty items in your inventory and elucidate your sourcing strategy.

Sales and Marketing: Articulate your sales and marketing strategies in detail. How will you entice and retain customers? Detail your advertising campaigns, promotional tactics, and the channels you'll employ to reach your audience effectively.

Funding Request: If you're seeking external financing, elucidate your funding needs. Specify precisely how you intend to allocate these funds and outline the terms you're seeking from potential investors or lenders.

Financial Projections: Underpin your plan with meticulous financial projections. Include comprehensive income statements, balance sheets, and cash flow statements that extend at least three to five years into the future. These projections offer a tangible picture of your financial trajectory.

Appendix: Finally, compile any supplemental documents that buttress your business plan. This might encompass market research data, resumes showcasing the expertise of key team members, and essential supplier agreements.

Remember that your business plan isn't a static document; it should evolve alongside your business. It serves as a dynamic tool for strategizing, decision-making, and effectively conveying your vision to potential investors and stakeholders. With a robust business plan in hand, you'll be better equipped to navigate the dynamic appliance store landscape and steer your venture toward long-term success.

Chapter 3:
Legal and Regulatory Considerations

Starting and operating an appliance store involves navigating a complex web of legal and regulatory requirements. Understanding and complying with these rules is essential to ensure the smooth and legal operation of your business. In this chapter, we'll explore the key legal and regulatory considerations for your appliance store, including choosing the right business structure, obtaining permits and licenses, adhering to health and safety regulations, and managing taxation.

Choosing a Business Structure

One of the first decisions you'll need to make when starting your appliance store is choosing the right business structure. The structure you select will have implications for your personal liability, taxation, and how you can raise capital. Here are some common business structures to consider:

Sole Proprietorship: This is the simplest and most common form of business ownership. As a sole proprietor, you have complete control over your appliance store, but you are personally responsible for all business debts and liabilities. Your business income and expenses are reported on your personal tax return.

Partnership: If you plan to start your appliance store with one or more partners, a partnership structure may be suitable. Partnerships can be general partnerships (where partners share equally in profits and liabilities) or limited partnerships (where some partners have limited liability). Like sole proprietors, partners report their share of business income and expenses on their personal tax returns.

Limited Liability Company (LLC): An LLC provides a level of personal liability protection for its owners (called members). Members are typically not personally responsible for the company's debts and liabilities. LLCs offer flexibility in management and taxation, as they can be taxed as a sole proprietorship, partnership, or corporation.

Corporation: A corporation is a separate legal entity from its owners (shareholders). This structure offers the most significant personal liability protection, as shareholders are generally not personally liable for the company's debts. Corporations also have the advantage of attracting outside investors by issuing shares of stock. However, corporations have more complex tax and regulatory requirements.

Cooperative (Co-op): A cooperative is owned and operated by its members, who share in the decision-making and profits. Appliance store cooperatives are often formed by a group of individuals with a shared interest. Co-ops have unique governance structures and may be organized as LLCs, corporations, or other legal entities.

Choosing the right business structure is a critical decision that should align with your long-term goals and financial considerations. Consult with legal and financial advisors to assess the best option for your appliance store.

Permits and Licenses

Running an appliance store requires various permits and licenses to comply with local, state, and federal regulations. These licenses and permits demonstrate that your store meets specific health, safety, and operational standards. Here's an overview of the essential permits and licenses you may need:

Business License: Most cities or municipalities require businesses to obtain a general business license. This license allows you to operate legally within a specific jurisdiction. The requirements and fees for business licenses vary by location.

Sales Tax Permit: Also known as a sales tax license or resale permit, this allows your appliance store to collect sales tax from customers on behalf of the state. It's necessary for selling taxable goods and services.

Building Permits: If you're constructing or renovating your store space, building permits are essential. They ensure that your construction plans comply with local building codes, safety standards, and zoning regulations.

Signage Permits: These permits are needed for any external signage you plan to install for your store. Regulations regarding size, placement, and type of signage vary by location and must be adhered to.

Occupational Permits: Depending on your locality, you might need specific occupational permits or licenses related to the appliance retail industry. These could include licenses for handling hazardous materials, operating power tools, or providing certain services.

Health and Safety Permits: If your store offers services like key cutting or tool repair, you might need health and safety permits to ensure compliance with regulations related to these services.

It's essential to research and understand the specific permits and licenses required in your area. Contact your local government offices or regulatory authorities to obtain detailed information about the necessary permits and the application process. Non-compliance with these regulations can result in fines, legal issues, or even the closure of your business. Therefore, ensuring that you have all the required permits and licenses in place before opening your appliance store is crucial for its legal and operational integrity.

Taxation

Understanding the taxation aspects of your appliance store is crucial for managing your finances and complying with tax laws. Here are key tax considerations:

Sales Tax: Most states and local jurisdictions impose sales tax on the sale of tangible goods. You are responsible for collecting and remitting sales tax to the appropriate taxing authorities. It's essential to understand the specific tax rates and exemptions that apply to appliance items in your area.

Income Tax: Your appliance store's income is subject to federal and state income taxes. The business structure you choose will determine how your income is taxed. Sole proprietors report business income on their personal tax returns, while corporations have separate tax obligations.

Employee Payroll Taxes: If you have employees, you must withhold and remit payroll taxes, including federal income tax, Social Security tax, and Medicare tax. Employers also pay a portion of these taxes.

Property Tax: Real property, such as the land and buildings housing your appliance store, is subject to property tax. The amount of property tax you pay depends on the assessed value of your property and local tax rates.

Licensing and Permit Fees: Some licenses and permits may have associated fees that must be paid on a regular basis.

Use Tax: If your state imposes a use tax, you may be required to pay it on items purchased out of state for use in your business.

Business Deductions: Take advantage of tax deductions available to appliance stores. These may include deductions for business expenses such as rent, utilities, advertising, and employee salaries.

Accounting and Recordkeeping: Maintain accurate financial records and accounting practices to facilitate tax compliance and reporting. Consider working with a certified public accountant (CPA) or tax professional to ensure accuracy.

Tax Credits and Incentives: Research if there are any tax credits or incentives available for appliance stores in your region. Some areas offer incentives for businesses that promote healthy eating or invest in energy-efficient equipment.

Filing Deadlines: Familiarize yourself with tax filing deadlines and make sure you submit all required tax forms and payments on time to avoid penalties and interest.

Navigating the complexities of taxation can be challenging, so it's advisable to consult with a tax professional or CPA with experience in the retail and appliance industry. They can help you maximize deductions, plan for tax liabilities, and ensure compliance with tax laws.

The legal and regulatory considerations for an appliance store are multifaceted and demand meticulous attention. Choosing the right business structure, obtaining the necessary permits and licenses, adhering to health and safety regulations, and managing taxation are fundamental aspects of running a successful and legally compliant appliance store. By investing the time and effort to understand and meet these requirements, you lay a solid foundation for the growth and longevity of your business.

Chapter 4:
Financing Your Appliance Store

Financing is a critical aspect of launching and sustaining a successful appliance store. In this chapter, we will explore the key elements of financing your appliance store, including estimating startup costs, securing funding from various sources, and managing your finances effectively.

Estimating Startup Costs

Before you kickstart your appliance store, figuring out the upfront investment needed is a must. Getting a good grip on startup costs not only helps secure the funding you need but also steers you clear of financial hiccups down the road. Here's what you'll need to factor in when crunching the numbers for your startup expenses:

Location Expenses: Tallying up what it'll take to snag and prep your store's spot, covering everything from rent or buying costs to renovations and snagging permits.

Gear and Setup: Calculating the expenses tied to getting your store decked out with essentials like handling equipment, shelves, cash registers, and those must-have point-of-sale (POS) systems.

Stock: Getting the initial load of products ready to roll in your store. The size and focus of your appliance store will play a role in how much this costs.

Permits and Papers: Setting aside cash for the necessary licenses and permits—things like health permits, business licenses, and any sign permits you might need.

Legal and Experts: Budgeting for legal aid, like hiring a lawyer to sort out your business setup and review contracts, plus any fees for consultants or advisors.

Getting the Word Out: Putting money aside for getting your store's name out there with marketing strategies and ads to drum up buzz for your opening.

Team Costs: Planning for bringing in and training staff during the startup phase. This covers salaries, benefits, and any recruitment costs.

Rent and Bills: Estimating what you'll shell out monthly for rent or lease, utility bills, and putting down security deposits.

Safety Nets: Making sure you've got cash on hand for business insurance—things like liability, property, and workers' comp coverage.

Tech and Tools: Setting aside funds for computer systems, software, and POS setups to keep sales and inventory in check.

Getting Started Funds: Having a stash for initial costs, whether it's beefing up inventory, paying staff, or keeping cash flowing while the store finds its feet.

Backup Cash: Prepping a cushion for any unexpected bumps or surprises that might pop up during the startup phase.

Launching the Buzz: Budgeting for events and marketing blitzes to hype up your store's grand opening.

Random Bits and Pieces: Factoring in those little costs that pop up, like office supplies, signs, or initial marketing materials.

Mapping out these costs in a detailed financial plan gives you a clear view of what to expect for startup expenses. Flexibility is key—be ready to tweak and adjust your budget as you gather more info and fine-tune your business plan.

Securing Funding

Once you have a clear understanding of your startup costs, the next step is to secure the necessary funding. Financing your appliance store may require a combination of personal savings, loans, investments, and grants. Here are some common sources of funding:

Personal Savings: Using your own savings to finance your appliance store is a common and straightforward approach. It allows you to maintain full control of your business and eliminates the need to pay interest on loans.

Family and Friends: Some entrepreneurs turn to family members or close friends for financial support. While this can be an accessible source of funding, it's crucial to formalize any agreements in writing to avoid misunderstandings.

Small Business Loans: Banks and credit unions offer various types of small business loans, including term loans, lines of credit, and equipment financing. These loans often require a solid business plan and collateral.

SBA Loans: The U.S. Small Business Administration (SBA) provides loan programs to support small businesses. SBA loans typically have favorable terms and lower interest rates, but they also involve a rigorous application process.

Investors: Seek investors who are willing to provide capital in exchange for equity or a share of the profits. Angel investors, venture capitalists, and private equity firms are potential sources of investment.

Crowdfunding: Crowdfunding platforms, such as Kickstarter and Indiegogo, allow you to raise funds from a large number of people online. This method is particularly effective if you have a unique and compelling business concept.

Grants: Some government agencies, non-profit organizations, and foundations offer grants to support small businesses, especially those focused on community development or sustainable practices.

Supplier Financing: Negotiate favorable payment terms with your suppliers. Some suppliers may offer extended payment periods, allowing you to manage cash flow more effectively.

Franchise Opportunities: If you're considering opening a franchise appliance store, the franchisor may provide financing options or assistance with securing loans.

Online Lenders: Online lending platforms offer various financing options, including short-term loans, business lines of credit, and invoice financing. These options may be more accessible for newer businesses.

Government Programs: Research local and state government programs that provide financial assistance, grants, or tax incentives to small businesses, especially those creating jobs or contributing to the local economy.

Alternative Funding: Explore alternative funding sources, such as merchant cash advances, factoring, or peer-to-peer lending. These options may be suitable for businesses with unique financing needs.

To secure funding successfully, you'll need to prepare a compelling business plan that demonstrates the viability and profitability of your appliance store. Lenders and investors want to see that you have a clear vision, a solid market strategy, and a realistic financial forecast. Be prepared to provide financial statements, cash flow projections, and any collateral if required.

Managing Finances

Managing the finances of an appliance store involves crucial steps that pave the way for stability and growth. To start, creating a detailed budget is key. This budget should cover all expenses, from inventory and rent to utilities, staff wages, marketing, and other operational costs. It acts as a guide, steering spending choices and maintaining financial discipline.

Keeping a watchful eye on cash flow comes next. Monitoring both incoming revenue and outgoing expenses is vital to ensure there's enough cash to handle day-to-day operations, pay suppliers, and deal with unexpected costs. Effective cash flow management prevents financial strain and keeps the business running smoothly.

Maintaining the right balance in inventory is critical too. Finding that sweet spot between stocking enough to meet demand without overstocking or understocking is essential. Smart inventory management optimizes cash flow and ensures popular items are available without tying up too much capital.

Managing accounts payable and receivable diligently is another aspect. Negotiating good terms with suppliers and making timely payments can positively impact cash flow. Similarly, efficient invoicing and following up on customer payments maintain a steady income stream.

Finding ways to save costs is also beneficial. Identifying areas where expenses can be cut without affecting quality or service can significantly boost profitability. This might involve renegotiating contracts, optimizing energy usage, or seeking more affordable suppliers.

It's wise to have a backup plan too. Setting aside funds for emergencies or unexpected expenses acts as a safety net during tough times, safeguarding the business against financial setbacks.

Lastly, seeking advice from financial experts or using accounting software can streamline financial management. Expert guidance helps in making informed decisions and tackling complex financial matters, ensuring the store's financial health and securing long-term success.

Chapter 5:
Store Design and Layout

The design and layout of your appliance store play a pivotal role in shaping the customer experience, optimizing efficiency, and driving sales. In this chapter, we will delve into the critical aspects of store design and layout, including store layout considerations, shelving and merchandising strategies, equipment and fixtures, and interior design.

Store Layout Considerations

Designing an effective store layout necessitates careful planning to create a shopping environment that caters to your customers' needs while optimizing sales. Here are several key store layout considerations:

Customer Flow: Plan a layout that guides customers smoothly through the store. Consider placing frequently purchased items towards the entrance to attract attention and encourage exploration deeper into the store. Create clear pathways that make it easy for customers to navigate and find what they need.

Product Placement: Organize products logically based on categories and usage frequency. Group related items together, such as plumbing supplies or electrical tools, to facilitate easy shopping and enhance the customer experience. Highlight popular or seasonal items prominently.

Aisles and Shelving: Optimize aisle width for easy movement and accommodate carts or trolleys. Adjustable shelving allows flexibility to accommodate various product sizes. Ensure shelves are well-stocked, neatly organized, and labeled clearly for effortless browsing.

Checkout Area: Strategically position checkout counters to minimize wait times and create a seamless checkout process. Consider additional displays near the checkout area for last-minute purchases or impulse buys.

Accessibility: Ensure the store layout is accessible to all customers, including those with disabilities. Maintain clear pathways, provide ramps or elevators where necessary, and ensure that product displays are reachable for all customers.

Safety and Comfort: Prioritize safety by keeping aisles clear of obstructions, ensuring proper lighting, and maintaining a clean and hazard-free environment. Incorporate comfortable waiting areas for customers and seating for those in need of assistance or consultation.

Flexibility and Adaptability: Design the layout with flexibility in mind to accommodate changes in inventory, seasonal displays, or promotional setups. This adaptability allows for easy modifications to meet evolving customer needs and store requirements.

Testing and Demonstration Areas: Consider allocating space for customers to test tools or equipment. Providing demonstration areas enhances customer engagement and allows for hands-on experience, influencing purchase decisions.

Employee Accessibility: Design employee workstations strategically to facilitate efficient restocking, inventory management, and customer assistance. Ensure staff areas are easily accessible but not obstructive to customer flow.

By considering these store layout considerations, you can create an inviting, efficient, and customer-friendly environment that maximizes sales potential and enhances the overall shopping experience at your appliance store.

Shelving and Merchandising

Effective shelving and merchandising are fundamental elements in the art of presenting products attractively, optimizing space, and ultimately driving sales. To achieve these goals, consider implementing the following strategies:

Shelving Types: Choose shelving that suits the variety of products in your store. Adjustable shelves allow flexibility for different-sized items, while specialized shelving, like pegboards or gridwall systems, cater to specific merchandise, such as tools or accessories.

Product Organization: Arrange products logically and aesthetically. Group similar items together, utilizing categories or project themes to guide customers. Use clear signage and labels for easy navigation and identification of products.

Planogram Implementation: Develop a planogram—a visual representation of how products are displayed on shelves—to optimize space and improve sales. It helps determine where products should be placed for maximum visibility and appeal.

Eye-Level Placement: Place high-demand or premium items at eye level to capture customer attention. This prime shelf space tends to attract more attention and encourages purchases.

Cross-Merchandising: Pair complementary items together to encourage multiple purchases. For example, display paintbrushes next to paint cans or lightbulbs near fixtures. Cross-merchandising encourages customers to buy related products in one shopping trip.

Seasonal Displays: Utilize shelving and displays to highlight seasonal or promotional items. Rotate merchandise based on seasons or upcoming holidays to capitalize on customer needs and preferences.

Visual Merchandising: Use visual techniques like color coordination, attractive displays, and well-organized shelves to create an appealing shopping environment. Incorporate informative signage or demo areas to educate customers about products.

Inventory Management: Regularly restock shelves to ensure products are readily available and well-presented. Implement inventory management systems to track stock levels and avoid out-of-stock situations.

Safety Measures: Ensure shelving units are sturdy, well-maintained, and meet safety standards to prevent accidents or injuries. Avoid overcrowding shelves to maintain a safe shopping environment.

Employee Training: Train staff on effective merchandising techniques and the importance of maintaining a well-organized and visually appealing store. Empower them to assist customers in finding products and providing product knowledge.

Effective shelving and merchandising strategies not only enhance the shopping experience but also contribute to increased sales, customer satisfaction, and a positive in-store atmosphere for your appliance store.

Equipment and Fixtures

When setting up an appliance store, acquiring the right equipment and fixtures is crucial for operational efficiency and creating an inviting shopping environment. Consider the following essential items:

Shelving and Racking: Invest in sturdy and versatile shelving units to display a variety of products. Adjustable shelves allow flexibility in accommodating different-sized items and adjusting layouts as needed. Racking systems are ideal for storing larger, bulkier items like lumber or pipes.

Display Fixtures: Use various display fixtures such as pegboards, gridwall systems, or slatwall panels to showcase tools, accessories, or smaller items. These fixtures offer flexibility in arranging merchandise and maximizing space.

Point-of-Sale (POS) System: Implement a reliable POS system to manage sales, track inventory, and process transactions efficiently. Choose a system that suits the scale and needs of your appliance store, integrating features like inventory management and reporting tools.

Storage Solutions: Invest in storage solutions like bins, drawers, or cabinets to organize smaller appliance items, fasteners, or parts. Clear storage containers with labels facilitate easy identification and access to inventory.

Cash Register and Checkout Equipment: Set up robust and user-friendly cash registers or POS terminals at checkout counters. Equip these areas with barcode scanners, receipt printers, and card payment terminals for smooth transactions.

Security Equipment: Install security systems like cameras, alarms, and theft deterrents to safeguard your store and inventory. Adequate lighting and visible security measures can deter potential theft.

Material Handling Equipment: Consider equipment like hand trucks, forklifts, or carts to handle heavy or bulky items. These aids streamline stocking, organizing, and moving merchandise around the store.

Signage and Display Materials: Utilize signage, banners, and display materials for product promotion, pricing, or highlighting special offers. Clear and informative signage guides customers and enhances their shopping experience.

Workstations and Tools: Equip workstations with necessary tools for providing customer service, cutting materials, or assisting with projects. Ensure employees have access to tools like saws, drills, or measuring equipment for store operations.

Lighting and Fixtures: Install adequate lighting fixtures to ensure a well-lit and inviting atmosphere. Use a combination of ambient, task, and accent lighting to highlight merchandise and create a comfortable shopping environment.

Choosing durable, functional, and visually appealing equipment and fixtures is integral to the success of your appliance store. Tailor these items to suit your store layout, customer needs, and operational requirements for a well-equipped and customer-friendly establishment.

Interior Design

Designing the interior of an appliance store is like crafting an experience for shoppers, where every element contributes to their comfort and convenience. The layout is a critical aspect, ensuring that aisles, displays, and checkouts are strategically placed for easy navigation and efficient operations.

Lighting plays a significant role, creating a welcoming atmosphere and showcasing products effectively. The right balance of natural and artificial light contributes not only to visibility but also to the overall sense of cleanliness and safety in the store.

Colors subtly influence the mood of the store. Warm and inviting tones create a comfortable ambiance, while strategic color use can highlight promotions or specific sections. Branding elements and signage add to the visual appeal and help customers easily recognize and navigate through the store.

Product displays are crucial for both aesthetics and sales. Well-organized shelves, attractive endcap displays, and eye-catching promotions draw attention to products and encourage spontaneous purchases. Grouping similar items together enhances the convenience of the shopping experience.

Checkout counters are central points of customer interaction. Designing these areas for efficiency and customer satisfaction, with features like express lanes and well-organized impulse-buy sections, contributes to a positive overall impression.

Incorporating technology adds a modern touch to appliance store design. Digital signage, interactive displays, and mobile checkout options not only enhance the store's appearance but also engage customers and make their shopping experience more convenient.

Safety and accessibility are paramount considerations in appliance store interior design. Ensuring adequate space for wheelchair users, clear emergency exits, and a well-designed customer service area contribute to an inclusive and secure shopping environment.

In essence, the interior design of an appliance store is a blend of functionality and aesthetics, aimed at creating a pleasant and efficient shopping experience. From the layout to lighting, colors, displays, and technology, each element plays a role in shaping the atmosphere and influencing customer behavior for the success of the store.

The design and layout of your appliance store are critical elements that influence customer experience, operational efficiency, and sales performance. By carefully considering store layout, shelving and merchandising strategies, equipment and fixtures, and interior design, you can create a shopping environment that attracts customers, encourages sales, and sets your appliance store apart from the competition.

Chapter 6:
Product Selection and Suppliers

The success of your appliance store heavily relies on the products you offer and the relationships you build with suppliers. In this chapter, we will delve into the critical aspects of product selection and suppliers, including building relationships with suppliers, managing inventory effectively, implementing pricing strategies, and considering private label products as part of your inventory.

Product Selection

Choosing the right products for an appliance store involves a strategic process that aligns with customer preferences, market trends, and business goals. The selection of products significantly impacts customer satisfaction, sales, and the overall success of the store.

To begin with, conducting thorough market research is crucial. Understanding consumer needs, preferences, and buying behaviors helps in identifying which appliances are in demand. Analyzing trends, such as the increasing popularity of energy-efficient or smart appliances, guides decisions on what products to include in the store's inventory.

Moreover, assessing the demographics and characteristics of the store's target market plays a pivotal role in product selection. Tailoring the product range to match the specific needs, lifestyles, and preferences of the target customers enhances the appeal and relevance of the offerings. For instance, catering to urban customers might involve stocking space-saving and technologically advanced appliances, while a focus on families might mean prioritizing durable and family-friendly products.

Another aspect of product selection is balancing between offering a variety of options and ensuring quality. Providing a diverse range of appliances that cater to different price points, brands, and features accommodates varying customer preferences. However, maintaining quality standards across the product range is essential to build trust and credibility among customers.

Staying updated with industry innovations and advancements is equally important. Keeping abreast of emerging technologies, new product launches, and changing consumer preferences allows the store to introduce innovative and trending appliances. This helps in staying competitive and meeting the evolving demands of customers seeking the latest features and functionalities.

Also, considering the supplier relationships and product availability is key. Establishing partnerships with reliable suppliers ensures access to a consistent and diverse range of quality appliances. Having a good understanding of the supply chain and product availability prevents stock shortages and enhances customer satisfaction.

The process of product selection for an appliance store involves a comprehensive understanding of customer needs, market trends, quality standards, and supplier relationships. Striking a balance between meeting consumer demands, offering diverse options, and staying updated with industry developments forms the foundation for a successful and appealing product lineup.

Building Relationships with Suppliers

Building strong and lasting relationships with suppliers is a crucial aspect of running a successful appliance store. These partnerships not only ensure a steady supply of products but also offer various benefits that can positively impact your business.

Exploring Suppliers for Your Appliance Store

The backbone of your appliance store lies in the suppliers you select. It's not just about products; it's about nurturing partnerships that align with your store's vision and goals.

Choosing suppliers is like uncovering treasures – seeking quality, value, and shared principles. Start your hunt by scouring online directories, industry associations, and networks specializing in appliance suppliers. Don't shy away from seeking advice from your network, tapping into contacts who might offer insider insights or valuable connections.

Consider crucial factors during your search. Location matters, ensuring timely deliveries and potentially cutting shipping costs. Quality is a must; your store's reputation relies on top-notch products. Finding the balance between quality and price is key; competitive rates without compromising on excellence.

Finding suppliers with values mirroring your business is vital. Whether it's a dedication to sustainability, ethical production, or a shared drive for innovation, these values lay the groundwork for a strong partnership.

Environmental impact is a significant consideration. Look for suppliers committed to eco-friendly products or reducing their carbon footprint, aligning with your store's values.

Seek out suppliers willing to support your venture, especially at the start. Some might offer flexible credit terms or trial-based discounts, aiding the launch and growth of your appliance store.

Your chosen suppliers become crucial partners shaping your store's success. Thorough research and deliberate selection pave the way for enduring partnerships that elevate your offerings and resonate with your customers.

Negotiating Supplier Contracts

After you've pinpointed suppliers that resonate with your appliance store's values and quality benchmarks, establishing supplier contracts solidifies the ongoing partnership. These contracts, often termed supplier agreements or product supply agreements, formalize the fundamental trade terms between your store and the suppliers. Whether adopting an existing agreement or crafting a custom one, these contracts lay the groundwork for a successful collaboration.

When crafting a supplier contract, it's crucial to encompass essential elements to safeguard both sides' interests. The contract should clearly outline:

Products and Services: Detail the precise products and services the supplier will provide, ensuring they align with your store's inventory needs and quality criteria.

Order Placement: Define the procedure for placing orders, including quantities, lead times, and any specific customization requirements.

Payment Terms: Establish explicit payment conditions, covering aspects like deposit amounts, discounts for early payments, processes for price adjustments, and accepted payment methods.

Delivery and Quality Standards: Specify delivery schedules, expected quality standards, warranties, and guarantees for received products. Include clauses addressing scenarios where products need installation or additional services.

Insurances and Indemnities: Outline insurance needs and the supplier's responsibility to compensate for losses caused by their actions or those of associated parties.

Intellectual Property and Confidentiality: Address ownership and protection of intellectual property rights for both parties, including confidentiality clauses to safeguard sensitive business information.

Dispute Resolution and Termination: Include provisions for resolving disputes, mechanisms for dispute resolution, and terms for contract termination, protecting both parties in unforeseen circumstances.

By meticulously addressing these components within supplier contracts, you establish a clear framework for a mutually beneficial and lasting relationship. The contract acts as a blueprint for collaboration, ensuring transparency, reliability, and accountability between your appliance store and its suppliers.

Building Strong Relationships with Suppliers
Once the agreements are sealed, the real effort begins to nurture and sustain these vital connections. Here's a roadmap to establish and maintain fruitful relationships:

Firstly, appoint a dedicated liaison within your team to serve as the primary contact for your suppliers. This ensures consistent and direct communication, fostering a relationship that extends beyond mere transactions. Having a designated point person streamlines interactions and builds familiarity, strengthening the partnership.

Transparency and integrity are foundational in supplier relationships. Keep communication channels open, addressing concerns or issues promptly and honestly. Upholding ethical conduct and fairness in your dealings builds trust, laying the groundwork for a lasting collaboration.

While challenges may arise, it's crucial to swiftly identify and communicate any product or service issues to your suppliers. This proactive approach not only resolves issues efficiently but also reinforces trust and reliability between both parties.

Managing financial commitments is integral. Stay vigilant about payment schedules and terms outlined in the agreement. Honoring financial obligations showcases professionalism and reinforces your reputation as a dependable partner.

In case internal challenges affect your ability to meet commitments, keep your suppliers informed. Transparently communicating issues, whether temporary cash flow problems or internal matters, fosters understanding and preserves the relationship.

Maintaining confidentiality is paramount. Refrain from discussing problems with external parties. Instead, seek guidance from trusted professionals like accountants, legal advisors, or business mentors for sensitive issues.

Lastly, schedule regular formal meetings, perhaps every 6 or 12 months, to review the partnership. These sessions offer a chance to discuss enhancements, future plans, and align objectives. It's an opportunity to acknowledge achievements, address hurdles, and ensure that both businesses are progressing in harmony.

Following these steps doesn't just establish a robust supplier network; it cultivates enduring partnerships that drive the success and growth of your appliance store.

Managing Inventory

Having secured suppliers and goods starts coming in, you would have to manage your inventories. Effective inventory management involves several key components that work together to ensure you have the right products in the right quantities at the right times.

One fundamental aspect of inventory management is accurate tracking. This entails keeping detailed records of your inventory levels, product turnover rates, and reorder points. Utilizing modern inventory management software can streamline this process, providing real-time insights into your stock levels and helping you make informed decisions.

Strategic purchasing is another crucial element. It involves ordering products in quantities that align with your store's demand patterns and sales trends. Analyzing historical sales data can help you forecast future demand and avoid overstocking or understocking items, which can tie up capital or result in missed sales opportunities.

Categorizing your inventory into different classifications can also be beneficial. Items can be categorized as fast-moving, slow-moving, or non-moving, allowing you to allocate resources more effectively. Fast-moving items may require frequent restocking, while slow-moving or non-moving items may warrant different management strategies, such as promotions or clearance sales.

Implementing inventory control measures can help prevent issues like theft, spoilage, or obsolescence. This can involve using security systems, monitoring expiration dates, and regularly inspecting inventory for damage or discrepancies.

Regularly conducting physical inventory counts is essential for accuracy. Periodic audits ensure that your recorded inventory levels align with the actual quantities on your shelves and in your storage areas. It's a time-consuming process, but the benefits in terms of accurate record-keeping and minimizing discrepancies are invaluable.

Effective inventory management also involves developing relationships with your suppliers. Establishing clear communication channels, negotiating favorable terms, and collaborating on supply chain efficiencies can help ensure a reliable and cost-effective flow of products into your store.

Finally, embracing technology can significantly enhance your inventory management efforts. Utilizing inventory management software, barcode scanning systems, and automated reorder triggers can streamline processes, reduce errors, and improve overall efficiency. Managing inventory in an appliance store requires a multifaceted approach that encompasses accurate tracking, strategic purchasing, categorization, control measures, physical counts, supplier relationships, and the integration of technology. By effectively managing your inventory, you can optimize your store's operations, maximize profitability, and provide a satisfying shopping experience for your customers.

Pricing Strategies

Pricing strategies serve as essential tools for boosting product sales and optimizing profits within an appliance store. Recognizing the significance of these strategies is paramount as they profoundly impact customer behavior, subsequently influencing the store's profitability and overall revenue. Finding the right equilibrium between competitive pricing, which attracts customers, and sustaining profit margins is vital for the long-term success of the business. This delicate balance ensures both customer satisfaction and financial stability, fostering sustained growth and prosperity for the appliance store.

Here are some pricing strategies:

Dynamic pricing is gaining traction, particularly in online appliance retail. It involves adjusting prices based on real-time data, such as demand, inventory levels, and competitor pricing. This strategy enables you to optimize prices according to market conditions, ensuring competitiveness and maximizing value capture. Think of your favorite ride-sharing app – it's a prime example of how dynamic pricing responds to changing demand. Implementing this approach can help your appliance store stay agile and align prices with market dynamics, enhancing competitiveness and meeting customer demand effectively.

One common pricing strategy is value-based pricing, where the store adds a markup to the cost of goods to determine the selling price. This approach ensures that the store covers its expenses and generates a profit. However, it may not consider market demand or competition, potentially leading to overpricing or underpricing.

Competitive pricing is another widely used strategy. In this approach, appliance stores set their prices in line with or slightly below the prices offered by their competitors. This strategy aims to attract price-conscious shoppers and maintain competitiveness in the market. Regular price monitoring and adjustments are essential to stay competitive.

Promotional pricing is a valuable tool to drive sales and customer loyalty. It includes strategies like discounts, buy-one-get-one-free (BOGO) offers, and loyalty programs. These promotions attract shoppers looking for deals and can boost sales for specific products or categories.

Psychological pricing tactics leverage consumer psychology to influence purchasing decisions. These tactics include using pricing endings like "$0.99" instead of rounding to the nearest dollar or emphasizing savings by showing a "discounted" price alongside the regular price. Such tactics create a perception of value and can lead to increased sales.

Price elasticity is an essential concept in pricing strategy. It measures how sensitive customer demand is to changes in price. Products with inelastic demand, such as essential tools, can tolerate price increases without significant decreases in sales. However, products with elastic demand, like luxury items, are more sensitive to price changes.

Strategic pricing should consider the overall store positioning and target market. A store focusing on premium or organic products may employ higher pricing to align with its brand image, while a store catering to budget-conscious shoppers may adopt a more aggressive pricing strategy.

Penetration Pricing is a strategic approach utilized by appliance stores when entering a new market. In this method, aggressive initial pricing is set for the products on offer. By presenting introductory lower prices, the store aims to entice price-sensitive buyers and establish a customer base seeking better value in products. However, it's essential to view this pricing strategy from a long-term perspective, ensuring profitability and sustainability over time.

In your appliance store, setting prices is an ongoing process that demands constant attention, analysis, and adjustment. By employing test and learn methodologies, you can experiment with diverse pricing strategies, assess their impact, and refine your approach accordingly. This iterative approach allows you to continuously improve and adapt your pricing strategies to the ever-changing market dynamics.

It's crucial to stay abreast of industry trends and keep a keen eye on competitor activities. Regularly monitoring your competitors' pricing strategies, promotional campaigns, and market trends offers valuable insights and opportunities for adjusting your pricing strategy. This competitive intelligence empowers you to make informed pricing decisions, ensuring your appliance store maintains a competitive edge in the market.

Utilizing effective pricing strategies like dynamic pricing, value-based pricing, psychological pricing, and penetration pricing can work wonders. These strategies help attract customers, add value to your offerings, and ultimately boost your profitability. It's crucial to tap into data-driven insights, keep an eye on market trends, and stay updated with industry shifts to consistently refine your pricing decisions.

Pricing isn't a one-time fix; it's an ongoing journey that demands flexibility and a bit of experimentation. By adopting these retail pricing strategies, appliance stores can adapt better to customer demands and the ever-changing market conditions. It's all about positioning your business for growth and success in this dynamic retail landscape.

Private Label Products

Private label products, often referred to as store brands or own brands, have become increasingly popular in the appliance industry. These products are created and sold exclusively by a particular retailer under their own brand name. Private label products offer a range of benefits for both retailers and consumers, and they play a significant role in the appliance store landscape.

One of the primary advantages of private label products is cost savings. Retailers can often produce private label goods at a lower cost compared to national or well-known brands. This cost efficiency allows retailers to offer these products to consumers at competitive prices, making them an attractive option for budget-conscious shoppers. Private label products also provide retailers with greater control over their product offerings. Retailers can tailor private label items to meet the specific preferences and demands of their target customer base. This customization allows for more flexibility in product development, ensuring that the products align with the store's brand image and customer needs.

Quality and value are key considerations for consumers when choosing private label products. Many retailers invest in stringent quality control and product testing to ensure that their private label items meet or exceed national brand standards. As a result, consumers often find private label products that offer a similar or even superior quality to their branded counterparts at a lower price point.

Private label products are not limited to any specific category; they can encompass a wide range of items, from food and beverages to household cleaning products and personal care items. This diversity allows retailers to create a comprehensive private label portfolio that covers various product categories, offering consumers an extensive selection of store brand choices.

Creating Your Private Label Product

Creating a private label product involves several key steps that allow businesses to offer unique products under their own brand. Here's an overview of the process:

Market Research and Product Conceptualization: Start by researching the market to identify gaps or opportunities where your private label product could thrive. Understand customer needs, preferences, and potential competition. Brainstorm product ideas that align with your brand and cater to a specific niche or demand.

Supplier and Manufacturer Selection: Find reliable suppliers or manufacturers capable of producing your envisioned product. Consider factors like quality, cost, production capacity, location, and their willingness to work with private label brands. Negotiate terms and establish a partnership that aligns with your requirements.

Product Development and Design: Collaborate with the supplier or manufacturer to develop the product according to your specifications. This involves designing packaging, creating product prototypes, selecting materials, and ensuring that the final product meets quality standards and reflects your brand identity.

Branding and Packaging: Develop a compelling brand identity for your private label product. Design packaging that not only protects the product but also resonates with your target audience. Consider factors like branding elements, messaging, labeling, and visual aesthetics that differentiate your product on the shelves.

Compliance and Regulations: Ensure that your product complies with industry regulations, safety standards, labeling requirements, and any other legal obligations in the regions where you plan to sell it. This might involve obtaining certifications or meeting specific guidelines for your product category.

Quality Control and Testing: Conduct thorough quality control checks and product testing to ensure that the private label product meets your standards for performance, safety, and durability. Address any issues or improvements before mass production begins.

Launch and Marketing Strategy: Plan a strategic launch for your private label product. Develop a marketing strategy that highlights its unique selling points, target audience, and channels for promotion. Utilize various marketing tools such as social media, influencers, advertising, and partnerships to create awareness and drive sales.

Distribution and Sales Channels: Determine the distribution channels through which you'll sell your private label product. Whether it's through your own website, e-commerce platforms, retail stores, or partnerships with other retailers, choose channels that align with your target market and brand positioning.

Feedback and Iteration: Gather feedback from customers and track sales performance to understand how your private label product is being received in the market. Use this feedback to iterate and improve the product, packaging, or marketing strategies to better meet consumer needs and preferences.

By following these steps, businesses can successfully create and launch private label products that resonate with their target audience, differentiate themselves in the market, and contribute to brand growth and profitability.

In recent years, private label products have evolved beyond just budget-friendly options. Many retailers have introduced premium or gourmet private label lines that compete with higher-end national brands. This expansion allows retailers to cater to a broader spectrum of consumers and capture a larger share of the market.

Successful private label strategies require effective branding and marketing efforts. Retailers must create a strong brand identity for their private label products to build trust and loyalty among consumers. They often invest in packaging design, advertising, and promotional campaigns to showcase the value and quality of their store brand items.

Private label products have gained traction globally, and consumers are increasingly open to trying these offerings. The growth of e-commerce has also provided a platform for retailers to reach a wider audience with their private label products, making them even more accessible to consumers.

Private label products have become a significant and dynamic segment of the appliance industry. They offer cost savings, quality, and customization for retailers while providing consumers with value and choice. As retailers continue to innovate and invest in their private label portfolios, these products are likely to remain a prominent feature in the appliance store landscape.

Chapter 7:
Staffing and Management

Effective staffing and management are fundamental to the success of your appliance store. In this chapter, we will explore the key components of staffing and managing your appliance store, including the hiring and training of employees, the creation of employee policies, scheduling and shift management, and performance evaluation.

Hiring and Training Employees

When establishing an appliance store, having the right team of employees is crucial for providing excellent customer service, managing operations, and fostering a positive shopping experience. Consider the following roles and personnel needed:

Store Manager: An experienced store manager oversees daily operations, manages staff, handles inventory, ensures customer satisfaction, and implements business strategies. They play a pivotal role in maintaining the store's efficiency and profitability.

Sales Associates: Frontline sales associates assist customers, provide product information, process transactions, and maintain a neat and organized sales floor. They should possess excellent communication skills, product knowledge, and a customer-oriented approach.

Cashiers: Efficient cashiers handle transactions, process payments accurately, and provide customers with a positive checkout experience. They should be proficient in operating cash registers and handling various payment methods.

Inventory Manager: An inventory manager oversees stock levels, conducts inventory audits, manages orders, and ensures accurate tracking of merchandise. Their role is crucial in maintaining adequate inventory levels and preventing stock shortages.

Technical Experts: Employ individuals with specialized knowledge in appliance, tools, or specific trades. These experts can provide valuable advice to customers, offer guidance on product selection, and assist with technical queries.

Customer Service Representatives: Customer service representatives handle inquiries, resolve issues, and address customer concerns promptly and professionally. They serve as the liaison between customers and the store, ensuring a high level of satisfaction.

Maintenance Staff: Maintenance personnel ensure the store premises are clean, well-maintained, and adhere to safety standards. They handle repairs, upkeep of equipment, and manage facilities to create a safe and pleasant environment for customers and employees.

The process of hiring and training employees begins with a well-planned recruitment process aimed at attracting candidates who align with your store's values and customer service standards. Utilizing various channels such as online job boards, local newspapers, and social media, you can advertise job openings effectively. Additionally, consider hosting in-person or virtual job fairs to engage potential candidates.

Once you've identified suitable candidates, a rigorous selection process, including resume screening, interviews, reference checks, and skills assessments, ensures that you select employees who not only possess the necessary qualifications but also fit well within your store's culture. When recruiting, prioritize individuals with relevant industry experience, a customer-centric attitude, strong communication skills, and a willingness to learn and adapt. Following the hiring process, invest in comprehensive training programs that encompass on-the-job training and formal training sessions. These programs ensure that your staff members are well-versed in product offerings, customer service expectations, safety protocols, and store policies.

Creating Employee Policies

Establishing clear and comprehensive employee guidelines is key to a smooth and happy workplace. Start by crafting an employee handbook that serves as a go-to guide for your team. This handbook should cover everything from work schedules and dress code to attendance rules and performance expectations. Be sure to outline a code of conduct that lays out expected behavior and ethical standards for everyone, stressing the importance of respecting both customers and fellow colleagues.

It's crucial to implement policies against discrimination and harassment to foster a safe, inclusive environment. Make sure to clearly explain reporting procedures so that all employees know their rights and how they're protected.

Safety and health policies should be a top priority, making sure you're in line with local regulations and emphasizing the importance of a safe work environment. When it comes to compensation, lay out everything transparently—wage rates, overtime policies, benefits, and perks. And don't forget about attendance and punctuality guidelines, including how to request time off or report absences.

Additionally, it's essential to create policies for handling conflicts, providing a fair and confidential process for employees to address any issues with management or coworkers. Lastly, educate your team on respecting customer privacy and confidentiality, making sure they're clear on how to handle sensitive information appropriately.

Performance Evaluation

Performance evaluation is a pivotal aspect of managing your appliance store staff. Define key performance metrics for various roles within the store, including sales targets, customer service ratings, and productivity goals. Provide ongoing feedback to employees, helping them understand their strengths and areas for improvement. Encourage open dialogue and constructive feedback as part of your organizational culture.

Conduct regular performance reviews or evaluations to assess employee performance against established metrics and goals. Set aside dedicated time for these evaluations and involve employees in goal setting to align their individual objectives with the store's overall objectives. Recognize and reward outstanding performance through incentive programs, awards, or bonuses to motivate and retain high-performing employees.

Moreover, discuss career development opportunities with employees and provide guidance on how they can advance within the organization. Offer training and support for career growth, demonstrating your commitment to their professional development. In cases where employees are not meeting performance expectations, develop performance improvement plans that outline specific steps for improvement. Offer support and resources to help employees succeed while also being prepared to take appropriate action, including termination, if performance issues persist despite efforts to address them.

Managing staffing and employee performance is an ongoing process that demands attention to detail, effective communication, and a commitment to fostering a positive work environment. By hiring and training employees effectively, creating clear policies, managing schedules efficiently, and conducting performance evaluations, you can build a motivated and capable team that contributes significantly to the success of your appliance store.

Chapter 8:
Marketing and Promotion

In the appliance industry, a well-crafted marketing and promotion strategy is essential to attract and retain customers, create a strong brand presence, and drive sales. In this chapter, we will explore the key components of effective marketing and promotion for your appliance store, including developing a marketing plan, establishing your store's branding and image, implementing advertising and promotion strategies, and utilizing loyalty programs to foster customer loyalty and engagement.

Developing a Marketing Plan

A marketing plan serves as the guiding blueprint for an appliance store's promotional activities, providing a structured approach to achieving desired outcomes. To develop a comprehensive marketing plan, several key steps should be followed.

Conducting Market Research

Market research forms the cornerstone of an effective marketing strategy for your appliance store. It's the vital process of gathering information that unveils the thoughts, purchasing behaviors, and geographical presence of your customers.

This research isn't just about understanding your customers; it's also a tool to craft an initial sales forecast, track market shifts, and keenly observe your competitors' actions.

By delving into market research, you'll gain valuable insights into what drives your customers' decisions, where they are located, and how they engage with appliance products. This knowledge becomes the bedrock upon which you can build a robust marketing strategy that resonates with your target audience, identifies growth opportunities, and sets your store apart from the competition.

Whether it's analyzing buying patterns, gauging customer preferences, or staying updated on industry trends, market research empowers your appliance store to make informed decisions and stay ahead in a dynamic market landscape.

Profiling Your Target Markets
Attempting to reach everyone with your appliance products can drain resources and yield minimal impact. Instead, focusing your marketing efforts through segmentation can be a game-changer. By grouping potential customers based on specific characteristics, you can refine and tailor your marketing strategies for maximum effectiveness.

Here are key segmentation factors to consider:

Geography: Understand where your customers live and work. This insight helps tailor your marketing approach to specific regions or areas.

Demographics: Consider gender, age, education level, occupation, and income. These details paint a clearer picture of your customer base and aid in crafting targeted messages.

Behavior: Why would they use your products? What draws them to your brand? Understanding usage rates and their preferred information sources guides how you communicate and engage with them.

Lifestyle and Values: Delve into their family situation, values, hobbies, and interests. Knowing these aspects helps align your marketing messages with what matters most to them.

Your ideal target market should not only require your appliance offerings but also be willing to invest in them. Understanding their needs, preferences, and behaviors empowers you to tailor your marketing efforts effectively. By honing in on specific customer segments, your appliance store can deliver tailored solutions that resonate deeply with these diverse groups, fostering stronger connections and driving more impactful results.

Crafting Your Unique Selling Proposition (USP)
Your appliance store's USP is the distinctive factor that sets you apart from competitors and entices customers to choose you over others. It's the essence of what makes your business shine in a crowded market. Defining and effectively communicating your USP is key to captivating potential customers.

To develop your USP, consider the following:

Passion for Products and Services: What excites you the most about your offerings? Your genuine enthusiasm often translates into a unique selling point. Whether it's the quality, variety, or innovation, conveying your passion can be magnetic.

Specialized Skills and Knowledge: Identify the unique expertise or knowledge your team possesses. This could be technical know-how, expert guidance, or a deep understanding of specific products—factors that differentiate you from the competition.

Customer Draw: Why do customers choose you over others? Understanding this helps define your USP. Whether it's exceptional service, a loyalty program, or a personalized approach, pinpoint what consistently attracts customers to your store.

Customer Benefits: Highlight the tangible advantages your customers gain by choosing your products or services. Whether it's convenience, reliability, cost-effectiveness, or solving specific problems, emphasize how customers benefit from their association with your store.

Key Messaging: When describing your business to strangers, what aspects do you emphasize? These points often align with your USP. Whether it's outstanding customer support, exclusive product lines, or a commitment to quality, these aspects become pivotal in shaping your USP's narrative.

By analyzing these aspects, you can distill your appliance store's unique strengths into a compelling USP. This proposition becomes the backbone of your marketing efforts, guiding your messaging, and resonating strongly with potential customers, ultimately setting you apart and driving customer loyalty and engagement.

Developing Your Business Brand
Creating a brand for your appliance store is a comprehensive endeavor that involves more than just the visual elements like logos and colors. It's about establishing a meaningful connection with your target audience. A well-crafted brand goes beyond surface-level aesthetics; it's a means to communicate your core values, your identity, and what customers can expect from your store.

Choose Your Marketing Media
When it comes to marketing your appliance store, the array of avenues available can be overwhelming. However, it's crucial to align your choices with your target audience to maximize their effectiveness.

Consider these options:

Business Website: Establishing an online presence through a website allows potential customers to explore your offerings, services, and values. It's a digital storefront that can attract and engage customers.

Social Media: Platforms like Facebook, Instagram, or LinkedIn offer opportunities to connect with your audience on a more personal level. Engaging content and interaction can build a community around your brand.

Blogging: Creating informative and valuable content through a blog can position your store as an authority in the appliance industry. It's a way to share expertise and attract customers seeking guidance.

Brochures and Flyers: Tangible marketing materials can be effective in local promotions or events. They provide a physical reminder of your store and offerings.

Networking Events: Engaging in industry-related events or local gatherings can help forge connections and establish your store within the community.

Print Advertising: Traditional print media, like newspapers or magazines, can still reach a specific demographic effectively, especially in localized markets.

Word of Mouth: Encourage satisfied customers to spread the word about your store. Positive recommendations can be a powerful driver for new customers.

Cold Calling: Direct outreach can be effective in B2B sales or when targeting specific customer segments. It's a proactive way to introduce your store and offerings.

Email Marketing: Sending targeted and personalized emails can nurture customer relationships, share promotions, and keep your store top-of-mind.

By understanding your target audience's preferences and behaviors, you can select the most fitting marketing avenues for your appliance store. Each avenue offers distinct opportunities to engage with customers, amplify your brand, and drive sales, so tailoring your approach to match your audience's preferences is key to maximizing your marketing efforts.

Establishing Goals and Allocating Budget for Your Marketing
Defining clear and concise marketing goals is pivotal for guiding your appliance store's growth. These goals should adhere to the SMART criteria—specific, measurable, attainable, relevant, and time-based.

Consider setting goals such as increasing website traffic by a certain percentage, boosting social media engagement, or enhancing sales of specific product categories within a defined timeframe. These objectives provide direction and allow for effective evaluation of your marketing efforts.

For an appliance store, these SMART objectives could encompass various goals:

- Increasing Sales: Define a specific percentage increase in sales within a set timeframe.
- Expanding Market Share: Set a goal to capture a certain percentage of the local appliance market within a year.

- Launching a New Store Location: Outline specific steps and targets to successfully launch a new store, including a timeline for pre-launch marketing, opening day sales, and post-launch growth.

Allocating a budget is equally crucial. Your marketing budget needs to encompass various elements essential for promoting your appliance store effectively. It should cover:

Website Development and Maintenance: Investing in a professional and user-friendly website is fundamental. Regular maintenance ensures it remains up-to-date and functional.

Search Engine Optimization (SEO) Strategy: Optimizing your online presence to rank higher in search engine results is vital for visibility. Allocate resources for SEO tools and strategies to enhance your store's online discoverability.

Branding Design: Designing a compelling brand identity, including logos, color schemes, and visual elements that resonate with your target audience.

Printing of Promotional Material: Costs related to producing business cards, brochures, signage, and other promotional materials that represent your store's image.

Advertising Costs: Funding for advertising campaigns across various platforms, whether digital, print, or local media.

Donations and Sponsorships: Consider community involvement through donations or sponsorships that align with your brand values and foster positive relationships.

Staff for Marketing Activities: Allocating resources for employing or training staff dedicated to marketing activities, ensuring a focused approach towards achieving marketing goals.

By establishing SMART goals and earmarking a comprehensive budget covering these critical marketing elements, your appliance store can strategically channel resources towards initiatives that align with your business objectives. This disciplined approach enhances the effectiveness of your marketing endeavors, leading to tangible results and the sustained growth of your store.

Nurturing Your Valued Customers
Your customers are the backbone of your appliance store's success, making it imperative to prioritize their care and loyalty. Exceptional customer service isn't just a bonus—it's a crucial factor that retains customers and sets you apart from competitors.

Here are strategies to cultivate customer loyalty:

Regular Communication: Engage customers consistently through social media, blogs, or e-newsletters. Providing valuable content and updates keeps your store top-of-mind.

After-Sale Follow-Up: Show your commitment by following up after a sale. Checking in on their satisfaction and offering support builds a lasting impression.

Delivering on Promises: Consistently meeting or exceeding promises made to customers establishes trust and reliability.

Going the Extra Mile: Surprise and delight your customers by providing benefits that surpass their initial expectations. It could be personalized recommendations, exclusive discounts, or exceptional service that leaves a lasting positive impression.

Utilizing Feedback: Embrace feedback and complaints as opportunities to enhance your services. Actively listening and implementing necessary improvements demonstrate your dedication to customer satisfaction.

Listening Intently: Take the time to genuinely listen to your customers. Understanding their needs and concerns helps tailor your services to meet their expectations effectively.

Staff Training: Invest in training your staff in customer service and sales processes. Equipping them with the skills to engage customers positively enhances the overall experience.

By implementing these strategies, your appliance store can foster a loyal customer base. Consistently providing exceptional service, actively listening to feedback, and going beyond expectations help create a strong bond with customers. This dedication not only encourages repeat business but also turns satisfied customers into enthusiastic advocates, driving positive word-of-mouth and contributing significantly to your store's long-term success.

Monitoring and Reviewing Marketing Effort

Regularly monitoring and assessing your marketing initiatives is crucial to ensure they align with your goals and deliver the desired outcomes, such as increased sales or heightened brand visibility. Initially, it's recommended to review your marketing plan every three months to ensure your activities are in sync with your overall strategy. As your business matures, consider reviewing the plan when introducing new products/services, encountering new competitors, or facing industry-related challenges.

Monitoring activities involves various assessments, such as regularly analyzing sales figures (monthly) or tracking customer engagement during advertising campaigns. Leveraging free analytic tools enables you to evaluate the effectiveness of your social media or website campaigns.

By routinely evaluating the performance of your marketing efforts, you can gain valuable insights into what strategies are yielding positive results and which ones may need adjustments. This process helps in optimizing your marketing activities, reallocating resources to high-performing channels, and refining strategies to better resonate with your target audience.

Additionally, staying vigilant regarding shifts in the market, new industry trends, or changes in customer behavior enables you to adapt swiftly. By continuously monitoring and reviewing your marketing plan, your appliance store remains agile and responsive to evolving market conditions, ensuring sustained growth and success in the competitive landscape.

Branding and Store Image

Branding encompasses more than just a logo and a catchy slogan; it represents the essence of your appliance store's identity. Building a strong brand image is not only essential for setting your store apart from competitors but also for fostering customer trust and leaving a lasting impression. To create a compelling brand identity, follow these essential steps:

Define Your Brand: The process begins by clearly defining your store's values, mission, and vision. What is it that you want your appliance store to stand for, and what unique qualities will distinguish it from others in the market?

Logo and Visual Identity: Craft a memorable logo and visual identity that align with your brand's personality and values. It's crucial to ensure consistency in these branding elements across all marketing materials and in-store signage.

Store Layout and Design: The interior design and layout of your store should seamlessly align with your brand image. The atmosphere, color schemes, and decor should vividly convey your brand's values and resonate with your target audience.

Customer Experience: Delivering a consistent and exceptional customer experience is pivotal to upholding your brand promise. Train your staff to embody your brand values in their interactions with customers, creating a lasting impression.

Brand Messaging: Develop compelling brand messaging that effectively communicates your store's unique selling points and resonates with your intended audience. Maintain the consistency of this messaging across all communication channels.

Brand Voice: Cultivate a consistent brand voice that reflects your brand's personality. Whether it's a friendly, informative, or humorous tone, ensure that it remains aligned with your brand image.

Community Engagement: Actively engage with the local community and support causes that align with your brand values. Sponsoring local events, participating in charity initiatives, or contributing to environmental efforts can enhance your brand's reputation and foster a sense of community.

Feedback and Adaptation: Continuously seek feedback from your customers to gain insights into their perceptions of your brand. Be willing to adapt and evolve your brand identity in response to changing customer preferences and market trends.

In essence, branding and store image creation involve a holistic approach that encompasses visual identity, messaging, atmosphere, and customer experience. By meticulously crafting and nurturing your brand, you can establish a distinct and memorable identity in the appliance market, leading to increased customer loyalty and trust.

Promoting Your Store

Getting the word out about your appliance store is essential, and fortunately, today's landscape offers a myriad of promotional avenues. Traditional business promotion methods remain effective, but the surge of social media has opened up a wealth of new marketing opportunities. Embracing digital marketing and social media can present affordable and accessible advertising options for your store. Here's how to leverage these tools to promote your business effectively:

Maximize Local Exposure

Harness the power of local listings by ensuring your appliance store is listed on Google—a modern-day equivalent to the classic yellow pages. Registering your business with Google offers numerous advantages, allowing potential customers to effortlessly locate your store's address and operating hours.

Here's why setting up a Google My Business account is pivotal:

Enhanced Visibility: A Google My Business account significantly boosts your store's online visibility. When users search for appliance stores in your area, your business will appear prominently in search results, increasing your chances of attracting local customers.

Ease of Access: Providing essential information such as your store's location, hours of operation, contact details, and even directions on Google Maps simplifies the process for customers to find and reach your store easily.

Customer Engagement: Google My Business facilitates customer engagement by enabling customers to post reviews and ratings of your appliance store. Positive reviews can enhance your store's reputation and influence potential customers' decisions.

Free Advertising: Utilizing Google My Business is essentially a form of free advertising. It extends your store's reach without incurring additional costs, making it a cost-effective way to increase your store's visibility online.

By setting up a Google My Business account, your appliance store can leverage the vast reach of Google's search engine to connect with local customers actively seeking appliance solutions. This simple yet powerful tool not only enhances your store's visibility but also facilitates customer engagement and trust, ultimately driving foot traffic and boosting your store's success in the local market.

Create a Truthworthy Website

Establishing a reliable online presence is vital for your appliance store. Your website should serve as a comprehensive hub showcasing your services, products, and the essence of your appliance ethos. It's not just about listing services; it's about conveying your appliance philosophy. Offer a seamless booking platform and foster communication with customers. Remember, your website often forms the initial impression of your store, so ensure it mirrors your brand values. Explore top appliance store websites for inspiration on how to best represent your business online.

Enhance Your Website with SEO Optimization

Boosting your appliance store's online visibility begins with optimizing your website's search engine optimization (SEO). SEO is the key to securing higher rankings in Google searches, making it easier for potential customers to discover your business online. While integrating relevant keywords across your web pages and blog posts is vital, effective SEO involves more than just keyword usage.

To optimize your website's performance on search engines, consider these steps:

Keyword Integration: Strategically incorporate relevant keywords throughout your website's content, ensuring they align with the products, services, and solutions your appliance store offers. Use tools or online resources to identify high-impact keywords for your industry.

Content Quality: Focus on creating high-quality, informative content that addresses common queries or issues within the appliance and home improvement sphere. Well-crafted content not only engages visitors but also attracts search engine attention.

Technical Optimization: Ensure your website is technically sound by optimizing loading speeds, mobile responsiveness, and user experience. A seamless browsing experience enhances your site's ranking potential.

Research and Learning: Expand your knowledge by exploring online resources or educational materials dedicated to mastering SEO techniques. Understanding the nuances of effective SEO practices can significantly impact your website's performance.

Professional Assistance: Consider hiring an SEO agency or consultant specialized in optimizing websites. Their expertise can offer tailored strategies to enhance your site's SEO, saving time and ensuring effective results.

By embracing SEO best practices, your appliance store's website can rise through search engine rankings, attracting more organic traffic and potential customers. A well-optimized website not only improves visibility but also establishes credibility and trust among online users, ultimately contributing to the success and growth of your appliance store in the competitive digital landscape.

Leveraging Social Media
Social media has evolved from a mere option to a crucial necessity for businesses. These platforms offer a dynamic space to inform, attract, and actively engage with your audience. Setting up a business account on most social media sites is entirely free, making it an incredibly cost-effective means of advertising for your appliance store. While creating paid posts and other forms of social media ads require an investment, the initial setup remains accessible to all.

By establishing a presence on platforms like Facebook, Instagram, Twitter, or LinkedIn, your appliance store gains direct access to a vast audience. Through regular posts, stories, and interactions, you can showcase your products, share valuable insights, and build a community around your brand. These platforms also facilitate two-way communication, allowing you to respond promptly to inquiries, address concerns, and foster meaningful connections with your followers.

Paid social media posts and advertisements offer additional advantages by targeting specific demographics, boosting visibility, and driving traffic to your store or website. Though these strategies involve a financial investment, they often yield measurable returns by reaching a tailored audience likely to engage with your appliance offerings.

Social media's versatility, accessibility, and potential to reach a wide audience make it an indispensable tool for your appliance store's advertising efforts. From establishing brand presence to engaging with customers and running targeted ad campaigns, leveraging social media enables your store to stay competitive, relevant, and connected in today's digital landscape.

Craft Compelling Content

Content stands as the linchpin for amplifying brand awareness and forging connections with your desired audience. Creating compelling and informative content—be it through blogs, video tutorials, or engaging infographics—serves as a powerful tool to showcase your appliance store's industry expertise and foster trust among your audience.

Blogs: Share valuable insights, tips, and trends related to appliance, home improvement, or DIY projects. Informative blog posts not only exhibit your knowledge but also provide practical guidance that resonates with your audience's interests and needs.

Video Tutorials: Capitalize on the visual medium by producing step-by-step video tutorials showcasing product demonstrations, repair techniques, or innovative uses of appliance items. These tutorials not only exhibit your expertise but also serve as valuable resources for your customers.

Infographics: Condense complex information into visually appealing and easily digestible infographics. Highlight product comparisons, maintenance tips, or creative project ideas.

Infographics serve as shareable content that can attract and engage your audience effectively.

By consistently crafting engaging and informative content, your appliance store can position itself as a trusted authority within the industry. This approach not only cultivates a deeper connection with your audience but also encourages them to view your store as a go-to resource for their appliance needs. As you offer valuable insights and guidance, you simultaneously bolster brand recognition and loyalty, fostering lasting relationships with your customers.

Use High-Quality Visuals

Visual content is the cornerstone of a compelling online presence. For your appliance store, investing in high-quality visual content for your website and social media platforms is paramount. In today's digital landscape, users often make decisions based on visuals, making it imperative to showcase your store in its best light.

Consider incorporating photos or videos that spotlight your products, services, facilities, and even your staff. High-resolution images showcasing the details and features of your appliance products can captivate potential customers, influencing their buying decisions. Additionally, videos demonstrating the usage or benefits of specific tools or equipment can be incredibly engaging and informative.

On social media, where attention spans are shorter, visually appealing content stands out. Striking images or eye-catching videos are more likely to capture users' attention and encourage engagement. Visuals have the power to convey your store's personality, professionalism, and the value you offer to customers.

Moreover, high-quality visuals not only attract attention but also contribute to establishing credibility and trust. They showcase your dedication to quality and attention to detail, which can resonate positively with your audience.

By prioritizing high-quality visual content across your online platforms, you're not just showcasing your appliance store; you're creating an immersive and compelling experience that entices potential customers to explore your offerings further. Visuals serve as a powerful tool to communicate the uniqueness and value of your store, setting you apart and fostering a strong connection with your audience.

Participate in Local and Community Events
For an appliance store deeply rooted in the local community, participating in both virtual and in-person events holds immense value. These gatherings offer prime opportunities to connect with your target audience, network with fellow business owners, and engage directly with potential customers, creating meaningful interactions that go beyond traditional advertising.

By actively participating in local events, you position your appliance store in the heart of the community, fostering relationships and strengthening your brand presence. Here's how these events can benefit your business:

Networking Opportunities: Events provide a platform to meet and collaborate with other local business owners, fostering partnerships that can mutually benefit each other's endeavors.

Direct Customer Interaction: Engaging with prospective customers face-to-face allows for personal connections. It's an ideal setting to showcase your products, share expertise, and address inquiries, thereby building trust and credibility.

Promotional Platform: Use these events as a promotional avenue to highlight special offers, exclusive deals, or upcoming products. Create a booth or display that captivates attendees and showcases the uniqueness of your appliance store.

Community Integration: Participation in local events signifies your store's commitment to the community. It's an opportunity to support community initiatives, establish goodwill, and solidify your store's position as a valued local establishment.

Whether it's setting up a booth at a local fair, sponsoring a community event, or engaging in online forums, actively participating in local and community events aligns your appliance store with the community's pulse. It's a chance to connect personally, forge meaningful relationships, and imprint your brand in the minds of local residents, ultimately contributing to long-term loyalty and success within your community.

Paid Advertising Strategies
If you're aiming to expand your appliance store's reach rapidly, investing in paid advertising can be a game-changer. Here are some popular paid advertising methods to consider:

Television and Radio Ads: While a traditional approach, TV and radio ads offer extensive reach. They cover a broader audience but typically involve higher costs compared to other methods.

Promoted Social Media Posts: Transforming one of your store's social media posts into an ad allows for targeted promotion. You have the flexibility to select a specific audience, geographic region, and duration for running the ad. This method ensures your content reaches those most likely to engage with it.

Pay-Per-Click (PPC) Ads: This model charges you each time a user clicks on your ad. Platforms like Google offer PPC advertising, displaying your ad prominently at the top of search engine results for specific keywords you've chosen. It's a cost-effective way to target users actively searching for appliance-related products or services.

Each of these paid advertising methods offers distinct advantages. Television and radio ads provide broad exposure, while promoted social media posts and PPC ads enable precise targeting, ensuring your message reaches the most relevant audience.

By strategically investing in paid advertising that aligns with your appliance store's goals and target demographic, you can amplify visibility, drive traffic to your store, and generate valuable leads, ultimately contributing to the growth and success of your business.

Engage Your Audience with Workshops and Offers
As an appliance store looking to make a mark, consider hosting workshops or webinars to share your expertise and solidify your position as a knowledgeable authority in your field. These sessions, whether online or in person, serve as invaluable platforms to impart specialized skills or technical know-how. By sharing valuable insights, you not only educate prospective customers but also establish meaningful connections within your industry. Additionally, these workshops present an opportunity to collect contact information from attendees, nurturing relationships for potential future business.

Another effective strategy is offering discounted or free products/services. Introductory discounts and complimentary trials act as enticing incentives for new customers, sparking their interest in your offerings. Encouraging referrals through customer-exclusive deals can amplify your customer base while fostering a sense of loyalty. Moreover, providing free samples or trials allows prospective customers to experience the quality of your products or services without a financial commitment. This approach builds trust and allows your offerings to speak for themselves, creating a strong foundation for future business relationships.

Remember, combining these strategies can amplify their impact. Investing in your business dreams is crucial, and a business banking expert can guide you on leveraging a business banking account to maximize your business's potential. By integrating these tactics, your appliance store can elevate its visibility, foster trust with customers, and establish a solid foothold in the market, paving the way for sustained growth and success.

Chapter 9:
Operations and Logistics

Efficient operations and logistics are the backbone of a successful appliance store. In this chapter, we will explore the intricacies of managing daily store operations, optimizing supply chain management, controlling inventory, and ensuring quality assurance to deliver a seamless shopping experience to your customers.

Daily Store Operations

Running a successful appliance store involves a multitude of daily tasks and responsibilities that demand meticulous planning and execution. These operational processes are the backbone of the store's efficiency and customer satisfaction. Here's an overview of essential daily store operations:

Store Opening and Closing: Establishing clear opening and closing procedures is paramount to ensuring the seamless commencement and conclusion of each business day. These procedures encompass tasks such as securely unlocking and locking the premises, setting up enticing displays, and conducting closing inventory counts to maintain inventory accuracy.

Staff Scheduling: Crafting a well-structured daily staff schedule is critical for maintaining optimal staffing levels, especially during peak business hours. Efficient allocation of staff resources not only guarantees excellent customer service but also minimizes labor costs, contributing to overall operational effectiveness.

Customer Service: Prioritize customer service excellence by providing extensive training to your staff. This training should encompass welcoming and assisting customers, addressing their inquiries promptly, and ensuring a consistently pleasant shopping experience that fosters customer loyalty.

Checkout Process: Streamlining the checkout process is essential to minimize waiting times for customers. Implement efficient point-of-sale (POS) systems and provide comprehensive training to cashiers to facilitate swift and accurate transaction processing, enhancing customer satisfaction.

Store Maintenance: Regularly inspecting and maintaining the store's physical premises is crucial. This entails tasks such as routine cleaning, equipment maintenance, and promptly addressing any safety hazards to create a safe and pleasant shopping environment.

Merchandising: Ensuring that products are displayed attractively and that shelves remain well-stocked is pivotal in maximizing sales and customer engagement. Frequent restocking and strategic visual merchandising contribute to a dynamic and enticing shopping experience.

Order Fulfillment: If your store offers online and phone orders, it's imperative to efficiently manage order fulfillment. Timely processing and delivery or pickup of customer orders are essential for ensuring high levels of customer satisfaction and repeat business.

Security: Implementing comprehensive security measures, including surveillance cameras, alarms, and loss prevention strategies, is vital to protect against theft and to ensure the safety of both customers and employees. A secure shopping environment enhances customer trust.

Waste Management: Develop a robust waste management plan to effectively handle and dispose of both perishable and nonperishable items. This includes implementing recycling practices and adhering to environmental regulations, aligning your store with sustainable practices and responsible waste disposal.

The daily operations of an appliance store are multifaceted and intricately interconnected. Effective management of these operations is pivotal in providing outstanding customer experiences, maintaining store efficiency, and ensuring the overall success of the business.

Supply Chain Management

Supply chain management plays a crucial role in the efficient and effective operation of an appliance store. It involves the planning, coordination, and control of the flow of goods and information from suppliers to the store's shelves, with the ultimate goal of meeting customer demand while minimizing costs and maximizing profitability.

One of the key aspects of supply chain management for an appliance store is vendor selection and management. Choosing reliable and cost-effective suppliers is essential to ensure a steady and high-quality supply of products. Appliance stores often work with a variety of suppliers, including wholesalers, and distributors, to source products, packaged goods, and other items. Establishing strong relationships with these suppliers can lead to better pricing, timely deliveries, and access to unique products that can give the store a competitive edge.

Inventory management is another critical component of supply chain management for an appliance store. Balancing inventory levels to meet customer demand while avoiding overstocking or understocking is a delicate task. Advanced inventory management systems and technologies can help store managers track product levels in real-time, forecast demand, and automatically reorder products when necessary. This reduces the risk of product spoilage, stockouts, and excess inventory, which can eat into profits.

Efficient transportation and logistics are vital for ensuring that products move smoothly from suppliers to the appliance store's shelves. Appliance stores often have multiple distribution centers to receive and distribute products to individual store locations. Optimizing routes, scheduling deliveries, and using technology like GPS tracking can help reduce transportation costs and ensure on-time deliveries. Moreover, eco-friendly transportation practices can align with sustainability goals and reduce the store's carbon footprint.

In today's highly competitive retail landscape, data analytics and technology play an increasingly significant role in supply chain management for appliance stores. Collecting and analyzing data on customer preferences, sales trends, and inventory turnover can help stores make informed decisions about product assortment, pricing, and promotions. The use of RFID tags, barcodes, and advanced software systems can enhance inventory visibility, reduce errors, and streamline the replenishment process.

Effective supply chain management is essential for the success of an appliance store. It involves vendor selection, inventory management, transportation, technology, data analytics, and compliance with safety regulations. By optimizing these aspects of the supply chain, appliance stores can enhance customer satisfaction, reduce costs, and remain competitive in a dynamic and evolving retail industry.

Inventory Control

Inventory control is a crucial element of supply chain management that plays a pivotal role in various industries. It refers to the processes and strategies utilized by organizations to efficiently manage their stock of goods. Effective inventory control is essential for ensuring product availability, reducing carrying costs, avoiding stockouts, and optimizing overall business operations.

One of the primary objectives of inventory control is to find the right equilibrium between maintaining sufficient stock levels to meet customer demand and minimizing excess inventory. Excessive inventory can tie up valuable capital and storage space, increasing the risks of obsolescence and spoilage. Conversely, insufficient inventory can lead to stockouts, resulting in lost sales and customer dissatisfaction. Businesses employ inventory control methods to determine optimal stock levels for each product, relying on historical sales data, demand forecasts, and lead times.

Accurate and up-to-date record-keeping is fundamental to effective inventory control. This entails tracking the quantity, value, location, and movements of every item in the inventory. Modern businesses often utilize computerized inventory management systems that automate these tasks, offering real-time visibility into stock levels and facilitating rapid decision-making. These systems can generate reports on stock turnover rates, reorder points, and supplier performance, facilitating inventory control efforts.

The ABC analysis is a fundamental concept in inventory control, classifying products into categories based on their significance and value. "A" items represent high-value, high-priority products requiring meticulous monitoring and tighter control. "B" items hold moderate importance, while "C" items are low-value, low-priority products. This categorization enables businesses to allocate resources effectively, focusing efforts on managing the most critical items.

Inventory control strategies encompass various techniques for managing demand fluctuations and uncertainties. Safety stock, for instance, involves maintaining a buffer of extra inventory to account for unexpected demand surges or supply delays. Reorder points and economic order quantity (EOQ) calculations help determine when to reorder products to maintain desired stock levels while minimizing carrying costs. Just-in-time (JIT) inventory systems take an alternative approach, aiming to minimize inventory holding costs by receiving goods from suppliers precisely when needed.

Effective inventory control yields numerous benefits for businesses. It can reduce carrying costs associated with storage, insurance, and handling. It helps prevent overstocking, which ties up capital, and understocking, which results in missed sales opportunities. Furthermore, it contributes to stronger supplier relationships by providing accurate demand forecasts and ensuring timely replenishment orders.

Inventory control is an indispensable practice within supply chain management, aimed at striking a balance between optimal stock levels and minimal carrying costs. It involves the application of techniques such as ABC analysis, safety stock, EOQ, and JIT to streamline inventory management. By implementing effective inventory control strategies, businesses can enhance their overall efficiency, customer satisfaction, and financial performance.

Quality Assurance

Maintaining product quality is paramount in the appliance business. Quality assurance measures help ensure that customers receive safe and fresh products:

Quality Standards: Establish and communicate clear quality standards for all products, including freshness, appearance, and packaging.

Vendor Compliance: Work closely with suppliers to ensure they adhere to quality and safety standards. Regularly audit and assess supplier practices.

Regular Inspections: Conduct routine inspections of products, checking for any signs of spoilage, damage, or expiration.

Employee Training: Train employees on proper handling and storage of products to maintain quality throughout the supply chain.

Recall Procedures: Develop clear procedures for handling product recalls. Communicate recalls to customers promptly and efficiently.

Efficient operations and logistics, coupled with a strong focus on quality assurance, are essential for the success and sustainability of your appliance store. By carefully managing daily operations, optimizing your supply chain, controlling inventory, and ensuring product quality, you can provide a seamless shopping experience that keeps customers coming back.

Chapter 10:
Growth and Expansion

Expanding your appliance store business is a significant step toward increasing profitability and market presence. In this chapter, we'll explore various strategies for growth and expansion, including broadening your product line, opening additional locations, considering franchising opportunities, and exploring international expansion.

Expanding Your Product Line

Diversifying your product offerings can breathe new life into your appliance store and attract a broader customer base. Here's how to approach expanding your product line. begin with thorough market research to identify products in demand within your community. This step involves considering customer surveys, analyzing market trends, and assessing competitor offerings. By understanding what your customers want and what's currently popular, you can make informed decisions about which products to add to your inventory.

Strengthening your relationships with existing suppliers is crucial, and also seek out new ones to source the additional products you plan to offer. Building strong supplier partnerships ensures a consistent and reliable supply of new items, helping you maintain the quality and availability of your expanded product line.

As you expand your product line, it's essential to revise your inventory management strategies. This includes reevaluating your storage capacity, shelving layouts, and tracking systems. Adequate storage and efficient organization are key to managing a more diverse inventory effectively.

Your employees play a vital role in the success of your expanded product line. Ensure your staff is knowledgeable about the new products and can assist customers with inquiries. Consider providing specialized training where necessary to enhance their expertise and confidence when dealing with the new offerings.

Creating effective marketing campaigns is crucial to introducing the new products to your customer base. Utilize a mix of strategies, including in-store displays, digital advertising, and promotional events, to generate interest and inform your customers about the exciting additions to your inventory.

Once the new products are on the shelves, continuously gather customer feedback. This valuable input allows you to fine-tune your offerings and make adjustments based on customer preferences. Listening to your customers and responding to their needs helps ensure the long-term success of your expanded product line.

Expanding your product line can be a strategic move to grow your appliance store business. However, it should be approached systematically, with careful consideration of market research, supplier relationships, inventory management, employee training, marketing efforts, and ongoing customer feedback. By following these steps, you can effectively diversify your product offerings and attract a wider customer base while maintaining customer satisfaction and profitability.

Opening Additional Locations

Expanding your appliance store by opening additional locations can significantly increase your reach and market share. However, this endeavor involves a series of crucial considerations to ensure a successful expansion.

Location Selection: One of the most critical factors in opening new appliance store locations is selecting the right spot. Conduct thorough location analysis to identify areas with high foot traffic, underserved markets, or demographics that align with your target customer base. Understanding the local market dynamics and competition is essential in making an informed decision.

Legal and Regulatory Requirements: Before proceeding with a new location, it's vital to navigate the legal and regulatory landscape. Ensure you understand and comply with local zoning laws, permits, and regulations specific to the appliance retail industry. Failing to do so can lead to costly delays and complications.

Financial Planning: Create a comprehensive financial plan for the new location. This plan should include detailed projections of startup costs, operating expenses, and revenue expectations. Securing the necessary financing or capital to fund the expansion is essential to ensure a smooth launch and sustained growth.

Staffing: The success of a new store often hinges on the quality and readiness of your staff. Begin the hiring and training process well in advance of the opening to ensure that the team is adequately prepared to serve customers and manage operations. Consistency in service quality across all locations is key to maintaining your brand's reputation.

Supply Chain Management: Expanding to additional locations requires a reevaluation of your supply chain and logistics operations. Consider centralizing warehousing and distribution to ensure consistent product availability across all stores. Efficient supply chain management is crucial for minimizing costs and ensuring product freshness.

Marketing and Branding: Developing a solid marketing strategy is essential to introduce the new location to the community. Leverage your existing brand identity, but be prepared to customize it to the local market. Tailoring your marketing efforts to reflect the unique characteristics and preferences of the new location can help build a loyal customer base.

Monitoring and Evaluation: After opening, continuously monitor the performance of the new location. Establish key performance indicators (KPIs) to assess its success and compare it to your initial projections. Be prepared to make adjustments to operations, marketing, and staffing based on the data and feedback received to ensure the ongoing success of the new store.

In conclusion, opening additional locations for your appliance store can be a rewarding strategy for growth, but it requires careful planning and execution. By addressing location selection, legal requirements, financial planning, staffing, supply chain management, marketing, and ongoing evaluation, you can increase your chances of a successful expansion and enhance your market presence.

Franchising Opportunities

Franchising opportunities offer a unique avenue for business expansion and growth. This business model allows entrepreneurs to replicate a successful and established brand, concept, or product by licensing the rights to operate under the parent company's name and guidance. Here, we delve into the key aspects of franchising opportunities.

One of the primary advantages of franchising is the ability to tap into a proven business model. Franchisors typically have a track record of success, a well-developed business plan, and a strong brand identity. This can reduce the risks associated with starting a new business from scratch and increase the likelihood of profitability.

For entrepreneurs, franchising offers a level of independence while still benefiting from the support and resources of an established brand. Franchisees can leverage the franchisor's expertise in areas such as marketing, operations, and supply chain management. This support can be especially beneficial for individuals who may have limited experience in running a business.

Franchising opportunities also come with a ready-made customer base. Established brands often have a loyal following, which can translate into a steady stream of customers from day one. This can significantly reduce the time and effort required to build brand recognition and attract customers.

However, it's crucial for potential franchisees to carefully evaluate the terms and conditions of the franchise agreement. Franchise agreements outline the responsibilities and obligations of both the franchisor and the franchisee. These agreements often include details about fees, royalties, territorial restrictions, and operational standards. Prospective franchisees should seek legal and financial advice to ensure they fully understand the terms before committing.

Franchising opportunities extend to various industries, from fast food and retail to fitness centers and service businesses. The choice of franchise should align with the interests, skills, and financial capacity of the potential franchisee. Conducting thorough market research and due diligence is essential to select the right franchise that matches one's goals and resources.

Once a franchise is established, ongoing communication and collaboration between the franchisor and franchisee are critical.

Franchisees benefit from regular training, updates on best practices, and support in addressing operational challenges. Franchisors, in turn, rely on franchisees to maintain the brand's reputation and uphold quality standards.

In conclusion, franchising opportunities provide a pathway for entrepreneurs to enter the business world with the backing of an established brand and support structure. It offers a balance between independence and guidance, making it an appealing option for those looking to start their own businesses. However, due diligence and a clear understanding of the franchise agreement are essential to ensure a successful and mutually beneficial partnership between franchisor and franchisee.

Each of these growth and expansion strategies comes with its own set of opportunities and challenges. The choice of which path to pursue should align with your business goals, resources, and risk tolerance. Careful planning, market research, and a commitment to maintaining the quality and values of your appliance store are essential elements of successful growth and expansion in the highly competitive appliance industry.

Conclusion

Starting and running a successful appliance store is a challenging but rewarding endeavor. In this comprehensive guide, we have explored every facet of this journey, from the initial considerations of why to start an appliance store and whether it's the right fit for you, to the intricate details of market research, legal considerations, financing, store design, staffing, marketing, operations, and various expansion strategies.

The appliance store industry is a dynamic and competitive one, marked by changing consumer preferences, evolving technologies, and shifting market trends. To thrive in this environment, you must be adaptable, customer-focused, and committed to delivering a top-notch shopping experience.

Key takeaways from this guide include:

Understanding Your Market: Thorough market research is the foundation of your appliance store's success. Knowing your target audience, competition, and location dynamics will guide your business decisions.

Legal and Regulatory Compliance: Navigating the legal and regulatory landscape is crucial. Choosing the right business structure, obtaining permits, and ensuring health and safety compliance are non-negotiable steps.

Financing and Budgeting: Carefully estimate your startup costs, secure funding, and manage your finances diligently. Budgeting and financial planning are essential for long-term sustainability.

Store Design and Layout: A well-designed store layout, effective shelving, and attractive merchandising contribute to a pleasant shopping experience that keeps customers coming back.

Product Selection and Suppliers: Building strong relationships with suppliers, managing inventory efficiently, setting competitive prices, and exploring private label options are key to product selection and procurement.

Staffing and Management: Hiring and training a motivated team, establishing employee policies, efficient scheduling, and performance evaluation are essential for smooth store operations.

Marketing and Promotion: Developing a comprehensive marketing plan, building a strong brand image, implementing effective advertising strategies, and utilizing loyalty programs are vital for attracting and retaining customers.

Operations and Logistics: Managing daily store operations, optimizing supply chain management, controlling inventory, and maintaining quality assurance are the cornerstones of a well-run appliance store.

Growth and Expansion: Strategies such as expanding your product line, opening additional locations, exploring franchising opportunities, and venturing into international markets offer avenues for growth and expansion.

In the appliance store business, customer satisfaction is paramount. By providing a wide variety of quality products, exceptional service, and a seamless shopping experience, you can build a loyal customer base and position your store for long-term success.

Remember that success in the appliance industry requires ongoing adaptability, a commitment to innovation, and a dedication to maintaining the highest standards of quality and customer service. As you embark on this journey, may this guide serve as a valuable resource to help you navigate the challenges and seize the opportunities that come your way in the world of appliance retail. Best of luck on your path to building a thriving appliance store business.

www.ingramcontent.com/pod-product-compliance
Lightning Source LLC
Chambersburg PA
CBHW062347290526
45794CB00005B/2129